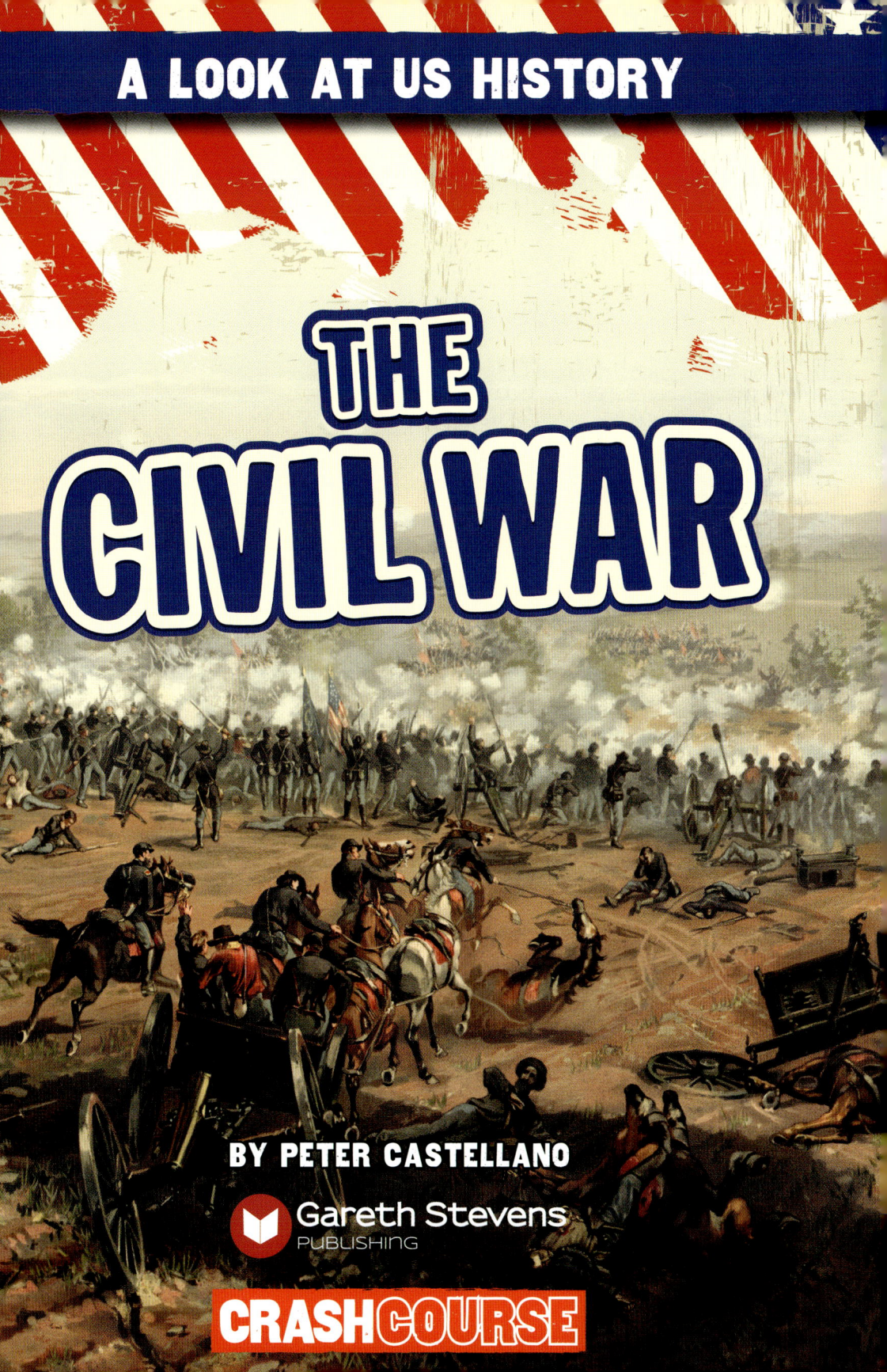

Please visit our website, www.garethstevens.com. For a free color catalog of all our high-quality books, call toll free 1-800-542-2595 or fax 1-877-542-2596.

Library of Congress Cataloging-in-Publication Data

Names: Castellano, Peter, author.
Title: The Civil War / Peter Castellano.
Description: New York : Gareth Stevens Publishing, 2018. | Series: A look at US history | Includes index.
Identifiers: LCCN 2016030668| ISBN 9781482460278 (pbk. book) | ISBN 9781482460285 (6 pack) | ISBN 9781482460292 (library bound book)
Subjects:  LCSH: United States--History--Civil War, 1861-1865--Juvenile literature.
Classification: LCC E468 .C27 2018 | DDC 973.7--dc23
LC record available at https://lccn.loc.gov/2016030668

First Edition

Published in 2018 by
**Gareth Stevens Publishing**
111 East 14th Street, Suite 349
New York, NY 10003

Copyright © 2018 Gareth Stevens Publishing

Designer: Samantha DeMartin
Editor: Kristen Nelson

Photo credits: Series art Christophe BOISSON/Shutterstock.com; (feather quill) Galushko Sergey/Shutterstock.com; (parchment) mollicart-design/Shutterstock.com; cover, p. 1 Adam Cuerden/Wikimedia Commons; pp. 5, 13, 23, 25 (both), 27 (both), 29 Everett Historical/Shutterstock.com; p. 7 H. P. Moore/Hulton Archive/Getty Images; pp. 9, 11, 21 Electric_Crayon/DigitalVision Vectors/Getty Images; p. 15 (flags) Santi0103/Shutterstock.com; p. 17 Heritage Images/Hulton Archive/Getty Images; p. 19 UniversalImagesGroup/Universal Images Group/Getty Images.

All rights reserved. No part of this book may be reproduced in any form without permission in writing from the publisher, except by a reviewer.

Printed in the China

CPSIA compliance information: Batch #CS17GS: For further information contact Gareth Stevens, New York, New York at 1-800-542-2595.

# CONTENTS

| | |
|---|---|
| At a Glance | 4 |
| Causes of the War | 6 |
| The Election of 1860 | 12 |
| Secession | 14 |
| Southern Advantages | 16 |
| The War Begins | 18 |
| The Proclamation | 22 |
| The Turning Point | 24 |
| The End of the War | 26 |
| Civil War Timeline | 30 |
| Glossary | 31 |
| For More Information | 32 |
| Index | 32 |

Words in the glossary appear in **bold** type the first time they are used in the text.

# AT A GLANCE

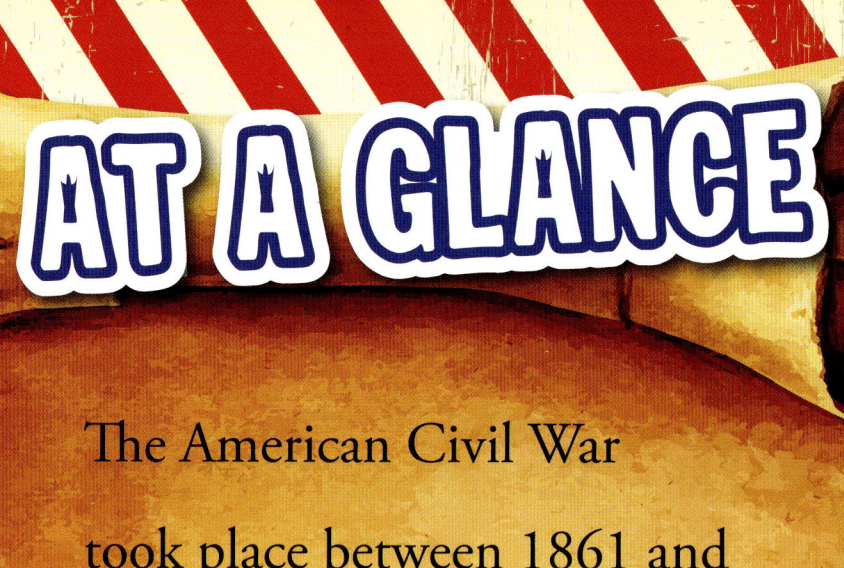

The American Civil War took place between 1861 and 1865. Sometimes called the "war between the states," the war set the Northern United States, called the Union, against a group of Southern states, called the Confederacy. It was fought wholly on US soil.

## MAKE THE GRADE

A civil war is a war between different parts or groups within the same country.

# CAUSES OF THE WAR

The Southern states' **economy** was based on farming. The North's was mostly based on factories. In 1828, Congress passed a high tax the South felt only benefited the North. A lower tax passed in 1832, but South Carolina voted to **nullify** the law anyway.

## MAKE THE GRADE

The South believed states' rights included the ability to nullify federal, or national, laws. The battle over states' governmental powers included other matters, too, such as slavery.

slaves planting sweet potatoes

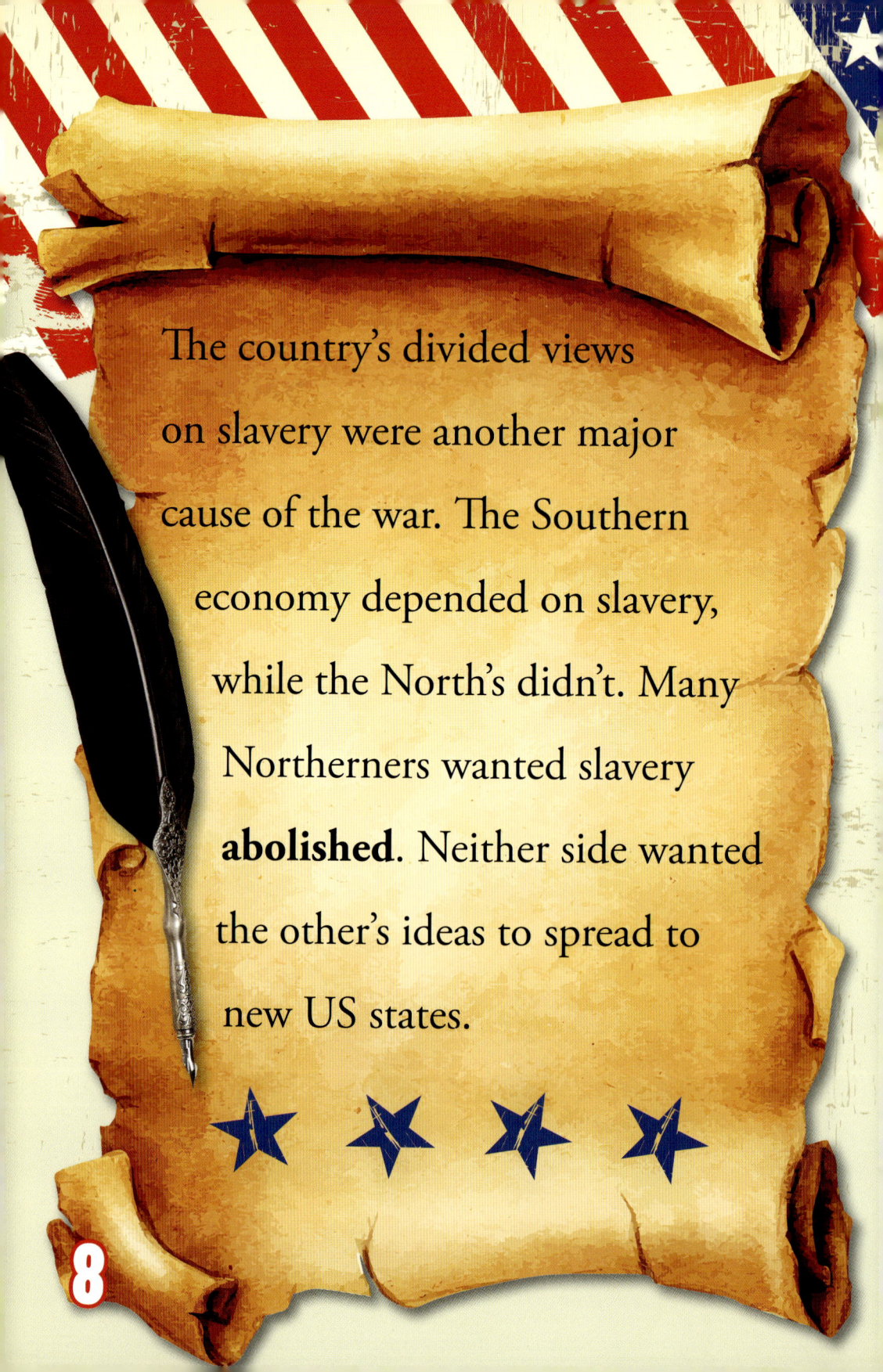

The country's divided views on slavery were another major cause of the war. The Southern economy depended on slavery, while the North's didn't. Many Northerners wanted slavery **abolished**. Neither side wanted the other's ideas to spread to new US states.

# United States, 1821

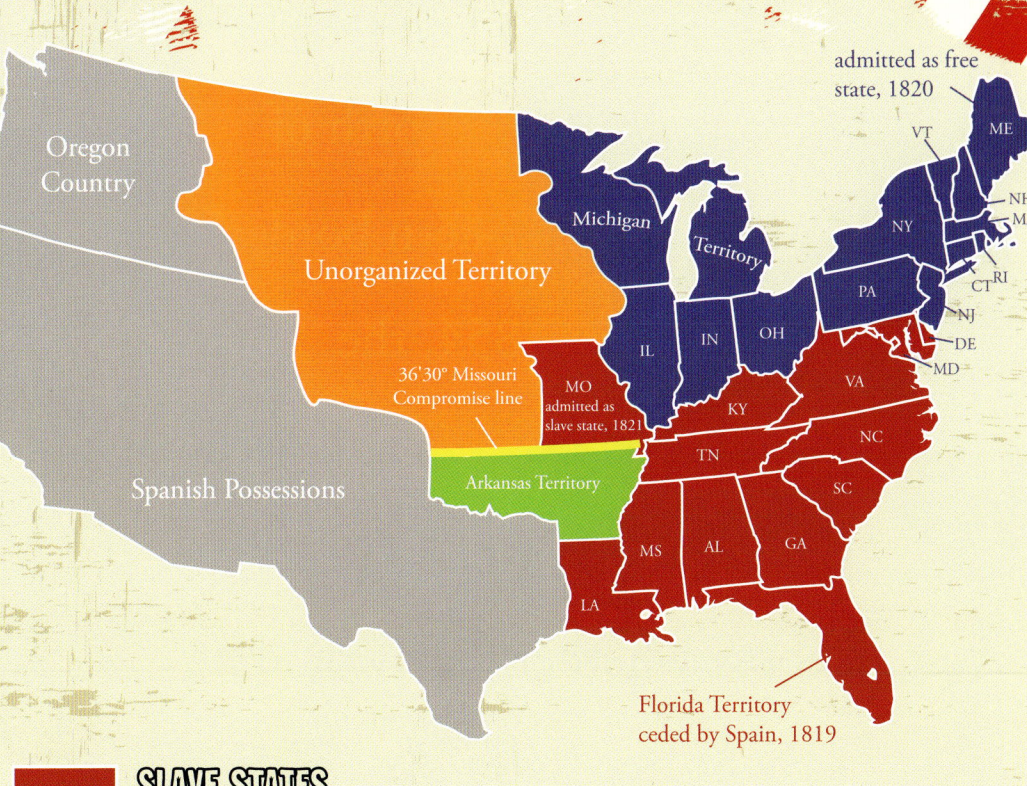

- **SLAVE STATES**
- **FREE STATES AND TERRITORIES**
- **CLOSED TO SLAVERY BY MISSOURI COMPROMISE**
- **OPEN TO SLAVERY BY MISSOURI COMPROMISE**

## MAKE THE GRADE

The Missouri Compromise of 1820 allowed Missouri to join the United States as a slave state only because Maine would join as a free state, or one that didn't allow slavery.

9

# THE ELECTION OF 1860

The United States remained together until the presidential election of 1860. Abraham Lincoln won, though he wasn't even on the **ballot** in the South! The North controlled Congress, too. The Southern states felt they had lost their say in the federal government.

## MAKE THE GRADE

Lincoln ran for president as a Republican, a group that opposed slavery and wanted to keep the country together.

# SECESSION

Lincoln's election was the last straw for the South. Seven states seceded, or left, the United States and formed the Confederate States of America. Jefferson Davis was chosen as the president of the Confederacy. By April 1861, four more states had joined them.

# MAKE THE GRADE

The rest of the world didn't recognize the Confederacy as an independent country. The world saw Lincoln as the leader of the United States and the Confederacy as a part of it.

## CONFEDERATE STATES OF AMERICA

- Alabama
- Florida
- Georgia
- Louisiana
- Mississippi
- South Carolina
- Texas
- Arkansas
- North Carolina
- Tennessee
- Virginia

## UNITED STATES OF AMERICA

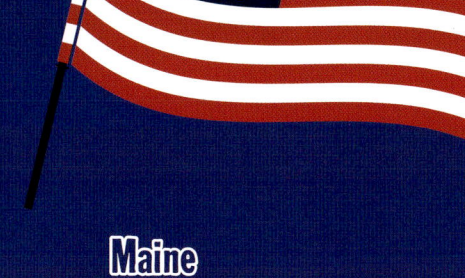

- Maine
- New York
- New Hampshire
- Vermont
- Massachusetts
- Connecticut
- Rhode Island
- Pennsylvania
- New Jersey
- Ohio
- Nevada
- Indiana
- Illinois
- Kansas
- Michigan
- Wisconsin
- Minnesota
- Iowa
- California
- Oregon

# SOUTHERN ADVANTAGES

The South had skilled military leaders. The Confederates also fought on land they knew well and were **defending** their homes. Furthermore, they were fighting for a cause—independence. However, the Union had the US Army, more people, and more railroads.

## MAKE THE GRADE

Four slave states didn't secede: Delaware, Kentucky, Maryland, and Missouri. They were called the border states.

# THE WAR BEGINS

On April 12 and 13, 1861, the Confederates took Fort Sumter in Charleston, South Carolina, from the Union army. By July, both sides had armies. They met on July 21 at the Battle of Bull Run. The Confederate army won, led partly by Colonel Stonewall Jackson.

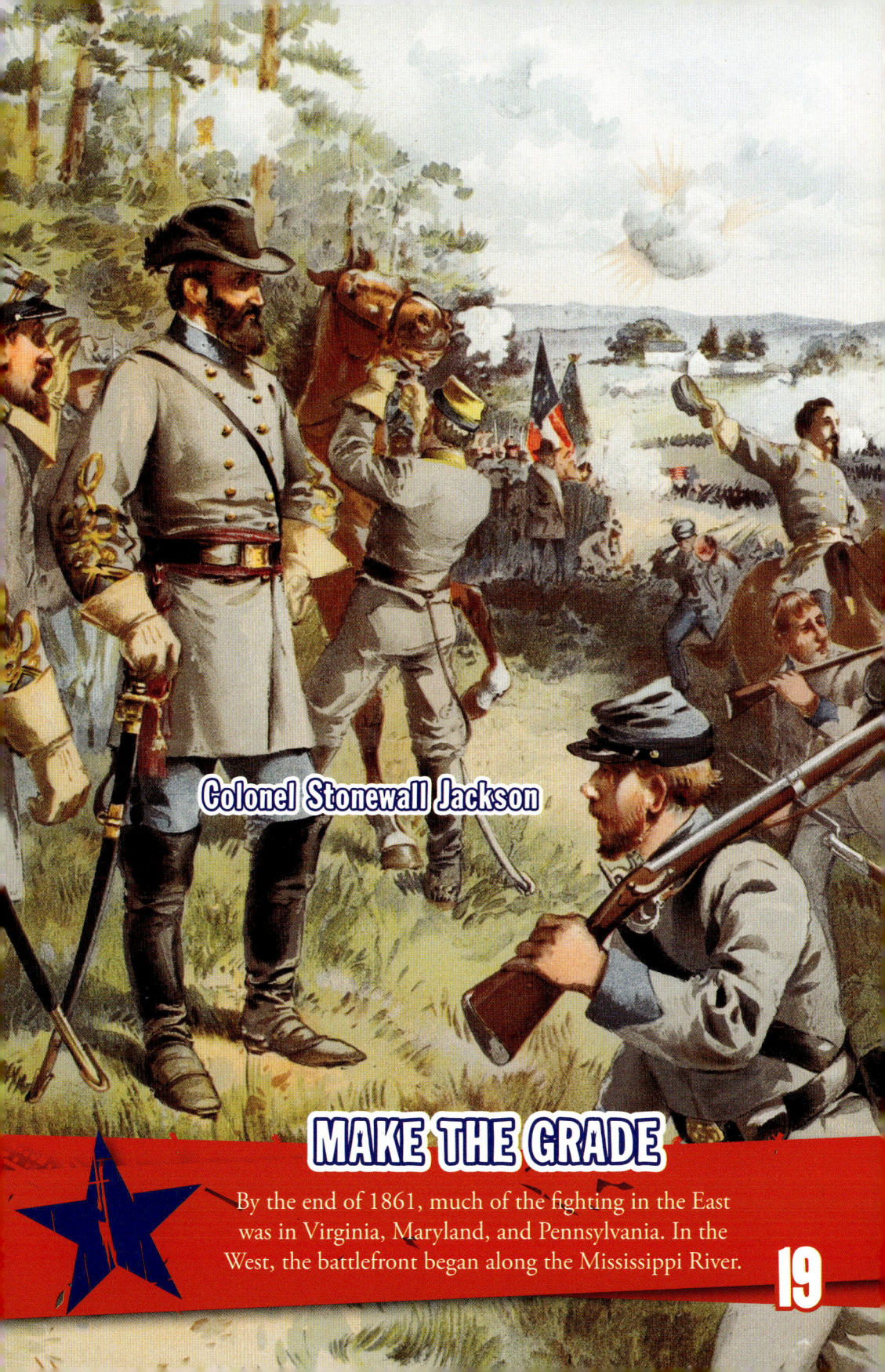

Colonel Stonewall Jackson

## MAKE THE GRADE

By the end of 1861, much of the fighting in the East was in Virginia, Maryland, and Pennsylvania. In the West, the battlefront began along the Mississippi River.

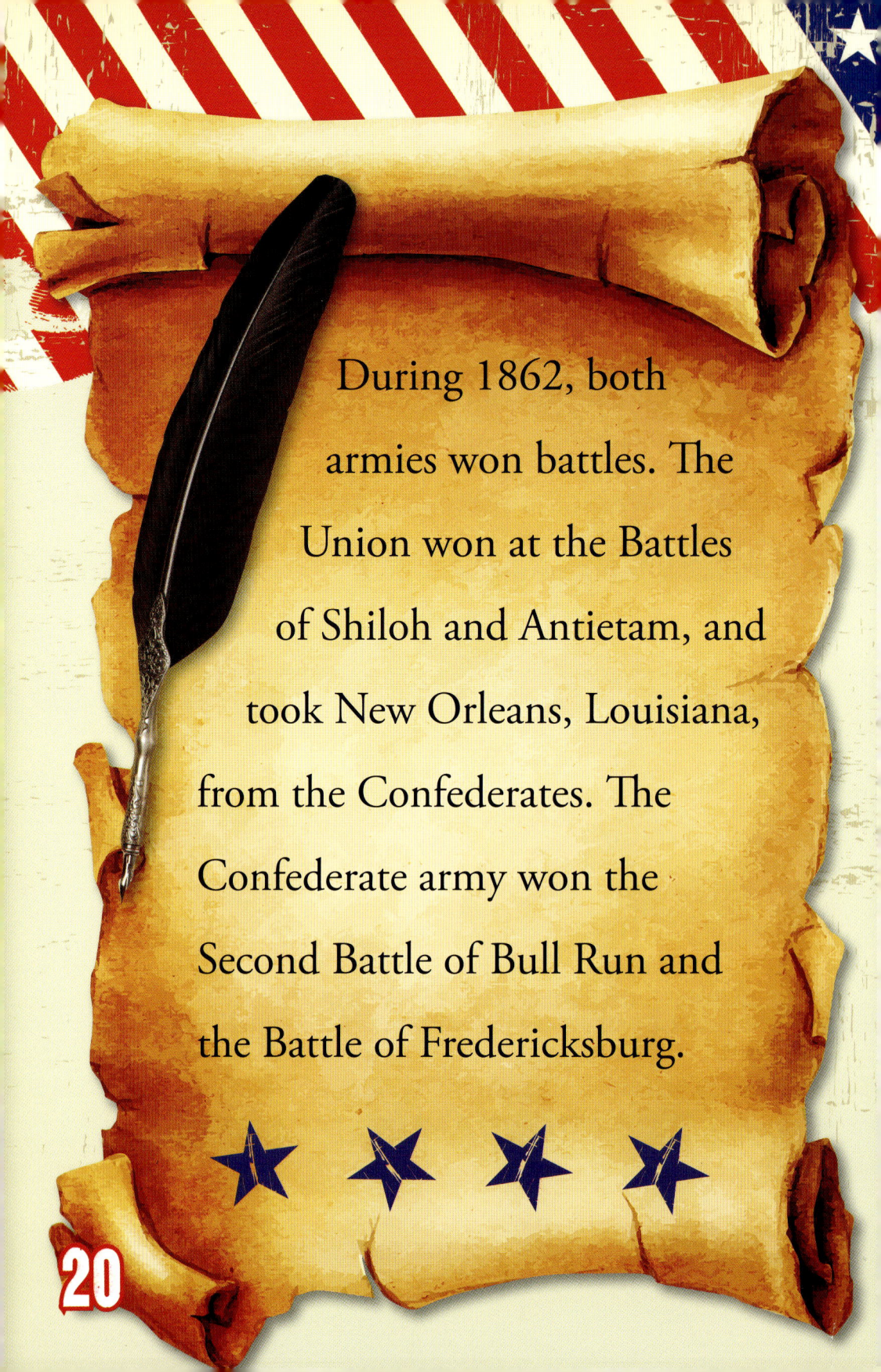

During 1862, both armies won battles. The Union won at the Battles of Shiloh and Antietam, and took New Orleans, Louisiana, from the Confederates. The Confederate army won the Second Battle of Bull Run and the Battle of Fredericksburg.

## MAKE THE GRADE

The Confederacy's *Merrimack* and the Union's *Monitor* were ships covered in iron. When they fought in March 1862, neither ship truly won the battle.

# MAJOR BATTLES OF 1862

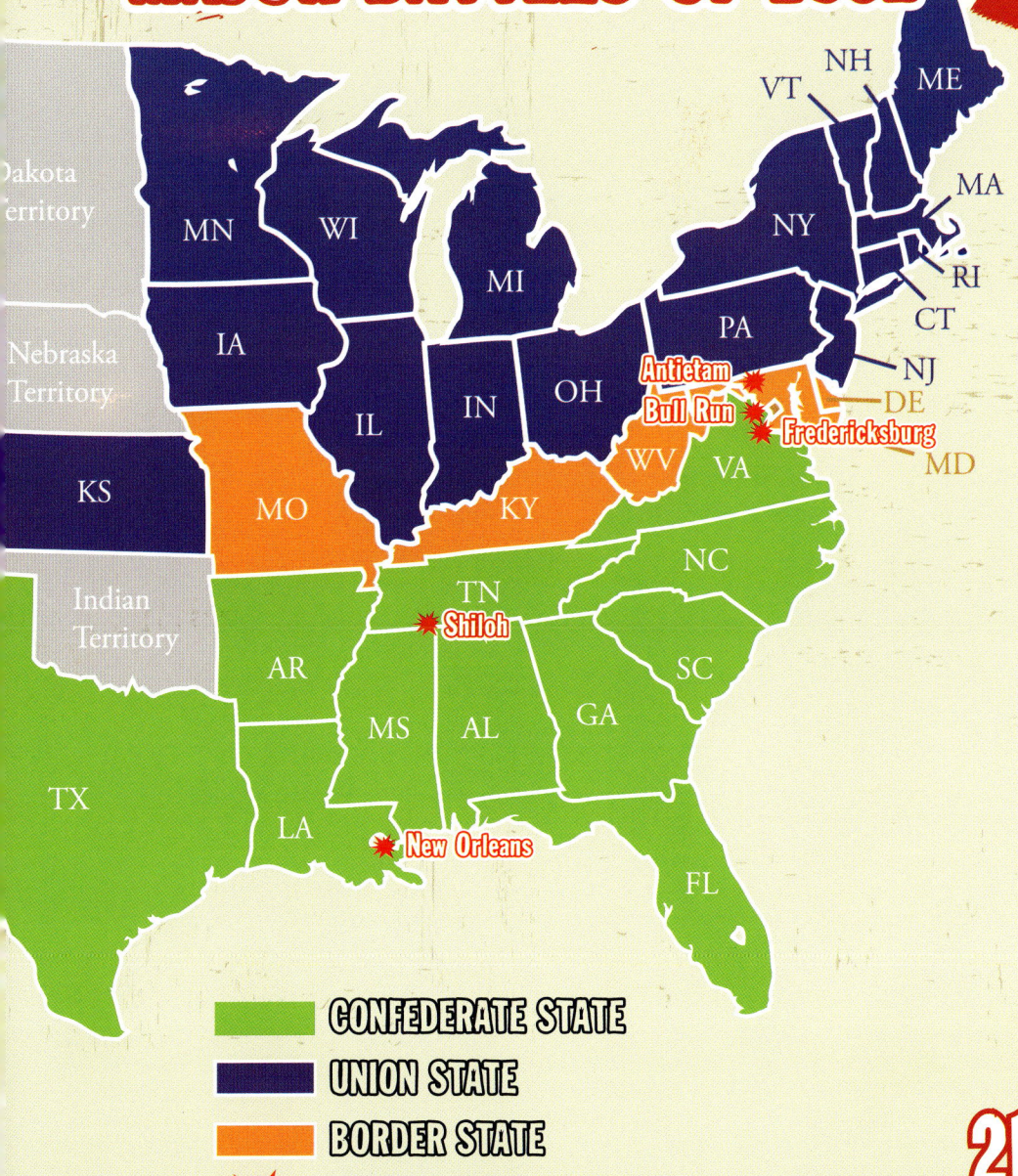

# THE PROCLAMATION

President Lincoln's goal during the Civil War was to keep the country together. Feeling **encouraged** by the Union's win at Antietam, he felt it was time to deal with slavery. In 1863, the Emancipation Proclamation freed all the slaves in Confederate states.

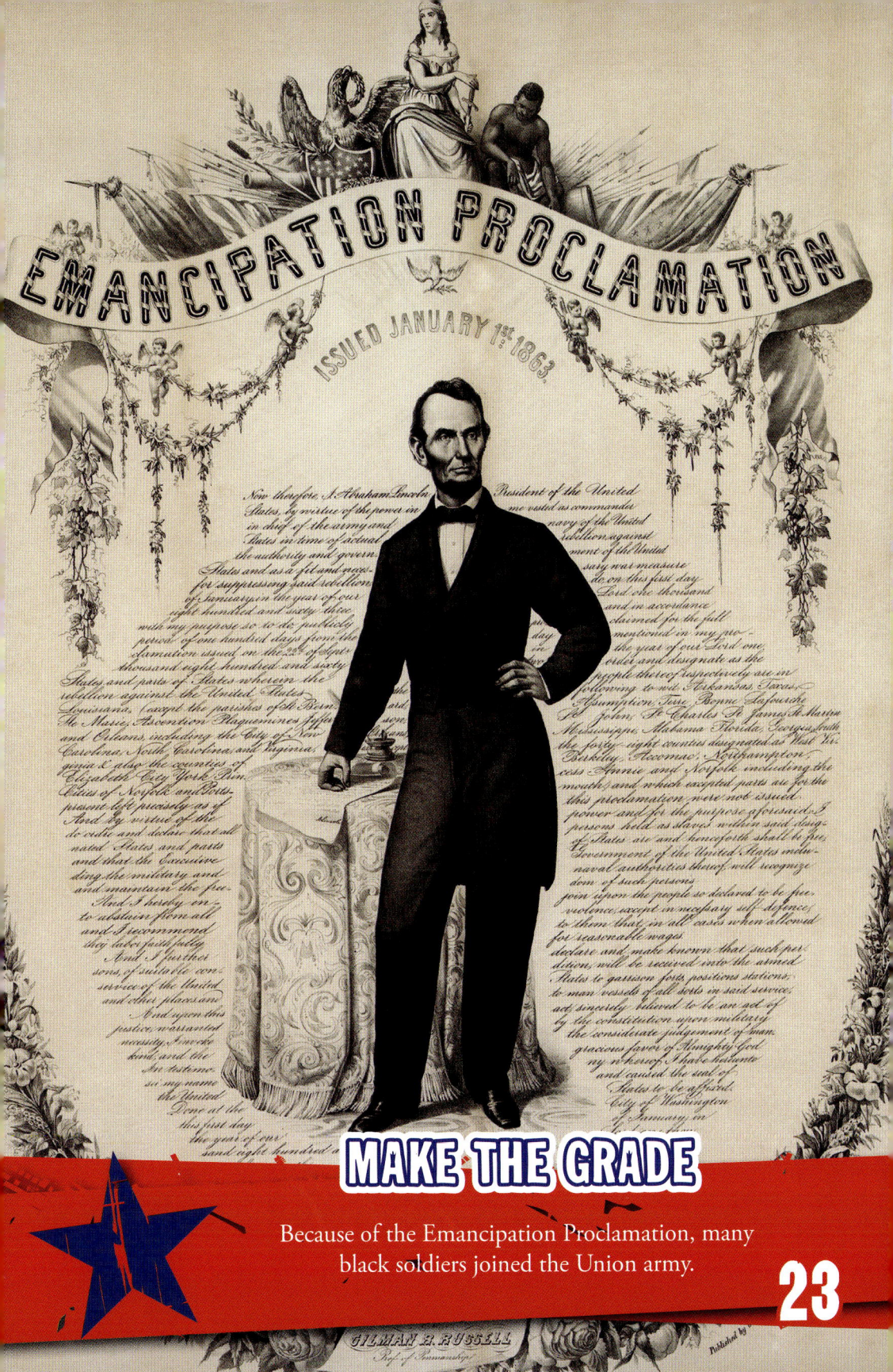

**MAKE THE GRADE**

Because of the Emancipation Proclamation, many black soldiers joined the Union army.

# THE TURNING POINT

Between July 1 and 3, 1863, the Union army stopped Confederate forces from **invading** the North in Gettysburg, Pennsylvania. The battle was the bloodiest of the war. The next day, the Union army won control of the whole Mississippi River in Vicksburg, Mississippi.

## MAKE THE GRADE

Ulysses S. Grant led the Union army at Vicksburg. Lincoln gave him command over the Union army in March 1864. He was a war hero and became president in 1869.

# THE END OF THE WAR

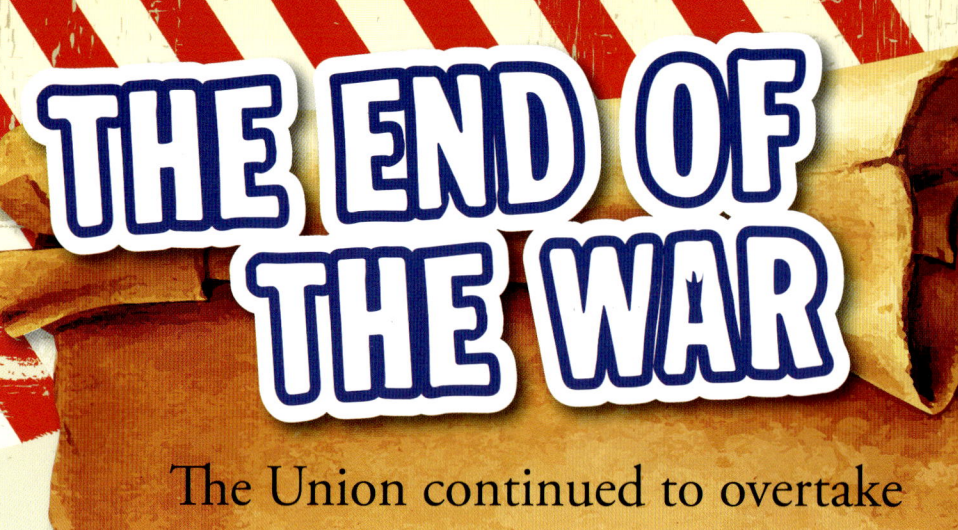

The Union continued to overtake Confederate forces into 1864. In June 1864, Grant began a **siege** on Petersburg, Virginia. Later that year, Lincoln won reelection. By 1865, Confederate general Robert E. Lee had few men and supplies. He gave up Petersburg on April 2.

# MAKE THE GRADE

Before the war, Lee was known to be a strong military leader. During the Civil War, Lee led Confederate forces to win many battles.

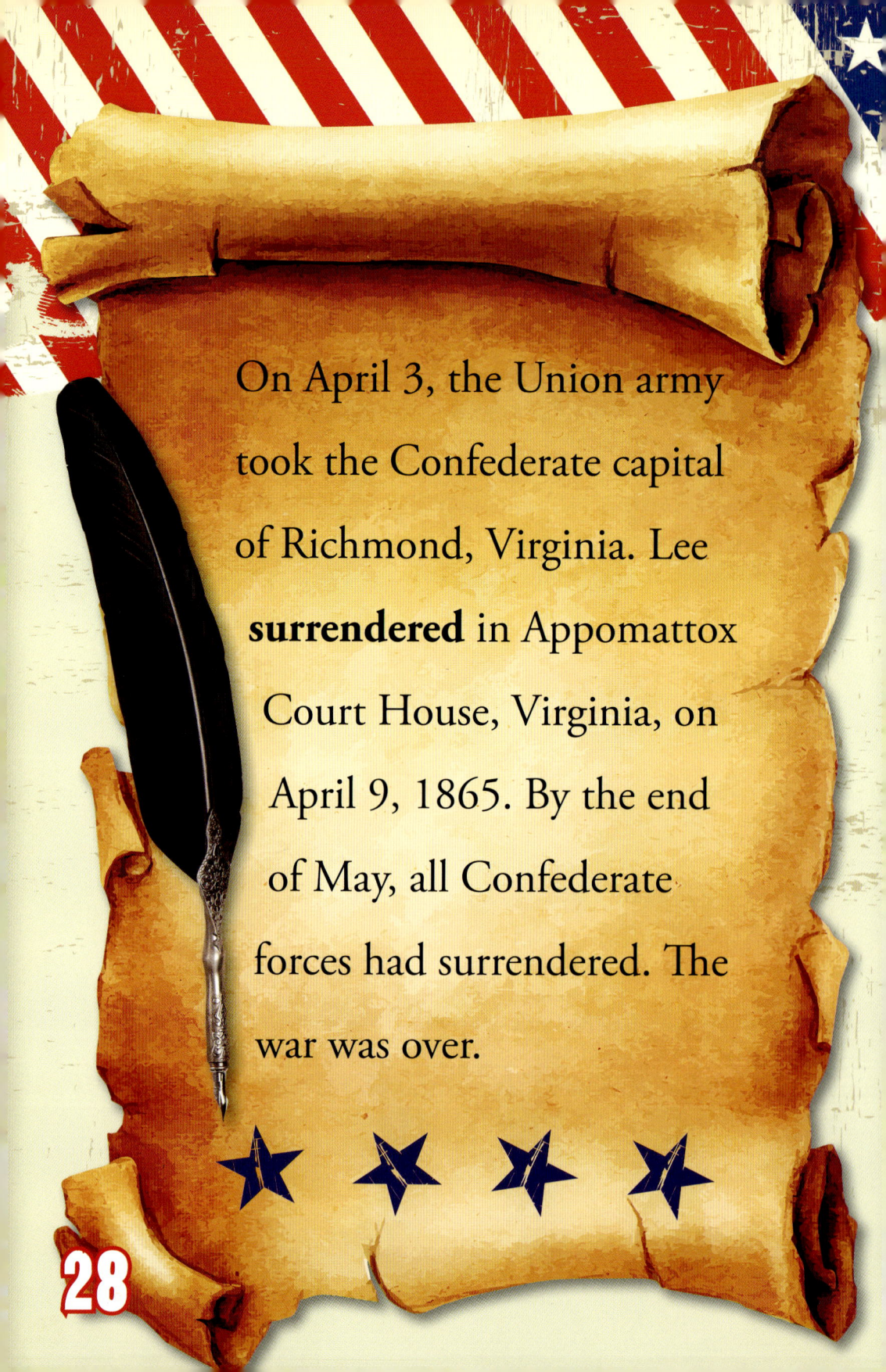

On April 3, the Union army took the Confederate capital of Richmond, Virginia. Lee **surrendered** in Appomattox Court House, Virginia, on April 9, 1865. By the end of May, all Confederate forces had surrendered. The war was over.

## MAKE THE GRADE

The period after the Civil War is called Reconstruction. During this time, seceded states were allowed back into the Union under certain conditions, and the South was rebuilt. Reconstruction lasted until 1877.

# CIVIL WAR TIMELINE

**November 1860**
Abraham Lincoln becomes president.

**December 20, 1860**
South Carolina secedes from the Union.

**February 8–9, 1861**
The Confederate States of America is founded.

**January 1, 1863**
The Emancipation Proclamation goes into effect.

**July 1–3, 1863**
The Battle of Gettysburg is the bloodiest of the war.

**July 4, 1863**
The Union army wins at Vicksburg, Mississippi.

**June 1864**
The siege on Petersburg begins.

**November 8, 1864**
Lincoln is reelected.

**April 2, 1865**
The siege on Petersburg ends.

**April 3, 1865**
The Union takes Richmond.

**May 1865**
Southern forces surrender. The war ends.

# GLOSSARY

**abolish:** to do away with

**ballot:** a sheet of paper listing names of those running for office and used for voting

**defend:** to guard against harm

**economy:** the money made in an area and how it is made

**encourage:** to give hope to

**invade:** to enter a place to take it over

**nullify:** to do away with a law

**siege:** the use of military to surround an area or building in order to capture it

**surrender:** to give up

# FOR MORE INFORMATION

## Books

Halls, Kelly Milner. *Life During the Civil War*. Minneapolis, MN: Core Library, 2015.

Lanser, Amanda. *The Civil War by the Numbers*. North Mankato, MN: Capstone Press, 2016.

## Websites

**The Civil War for Fifth Graders**
radford.edu/~sbisset/civilwar.htm
This website presents many details of the US Civil War in a reader-friendly, useful way.

**Publisher's note to educators and parents:** Our editors have carefully reviewed these websites to ensure that they are suitable for students. Many websites change frequently, however, and we cannot guarantee that a site's future contents will continue to meet our high standards of quality and educational value. Be advised that students should be closely supervised whenever they access the Internet.

# INDEX

Confederacy 4, 14, 15, 21
Confederates 16, 18, 20, 22, 24, 26, 27, 28
Confederate States of America 14, 30
Davis, Jefferson 14
Emancipation Proclamation 22, 23, 30
Fort Sumter 18
Gettysburg 24, 30
Jackson, Stonewall 18
Lincoln, Abraham 12, 13, 14, 15, 22, 25, 26, 30
Petersburg 26, 30
Richmond 28, 30
slavery 7, 8, 9, 10, 13, 22
Union 4, 16, 18, 20, 21, 22, 23, 24, 25, 26, 28, 29, 30
Vicksburg 24, 25, 30